SKYROCKET YOUR SUCCESS 2.0!

The Corporate Women's Road
Map To Navigate From
Employee To Entrepreneur!

QUEASHAR L HALLIBURTON

ISBN: (eBook) 979-8-218-12486-1
ISBN: (Paperback) 979-8-218-11910-2
Library of Congress Control Number: 2022923080

Book Cover Design: Arslan Naeem

Formatting: Jstuntpublisher on Fiverr

Publisher: QUEASHAR DETROIT PUBLISHING, LLC ®

P.O. BOX 201126
FERNDALE, MI 48220
For more information, please visit:
https://www.sharhalliburton.com.

Printed in the United States of America.

For free resources to help you navigate from employee to entrepreneur, visit
www.skyrocketwithshar.com/resources.

Table Of Contents

Acknowledgments _____ vii

Dedication _____ ix

Introduction _____ 1

Chapter One: Being Stuck Is No Longer An Excuse! _____ 7

Chapter Two: Tap Into Your Zone Of Genius!_____ 15

Chapter Three: Elevate Your Mindset For Entrepreneurship! _ 23

Chapter Four: Redefine Your Success Journey! _____ 37

Chapter Five: Incorporate, Build & Collaborate!_____ 45

Chapter Six: Launch Your Dream & Start Planning Your Exit!__ 59

Chapter Seven: Activate, Maintain & Sustain! _____ 69

Notes _____ 75

Epilogue _____ 87

References _____ 91

About The Author_____ 93

Acknowledgments

First, I must give honor to my Lord and Savior, Jesus Christ, for life, health, and strength. I'm grateful for the ability to pursue my God-given gifts that enable me to support and empower women to achieve greatness.

I thank my mother, Jarita R. Halliburton, for her support. I'd also like to thank my wonderful family and supportive siblings, Shergora, Lisa, Cornelius, Jr., and Kellie. I'd also like to thank my friend and accountability partner, Mona Reed, for always being a supportive friend with a listening ear as I push through many obstacles.

I appreciate my coaches, Charlotte Howard and Jasmine Womack & The Empact Group, who have pushed and supported me to ascend to new levels. Finally, I'd like to thank my Facebook family and friends for taking time from your busy schedules to reply to my Facebook survey posts. I love and appreciate you all, so I am giving you a shout-out below!

Adrienne R. Long
April Bonner-Archer
Arthur Halliburton
Ayana Powers
Brandy Jackson
Carol Manciel
Chastity Pratt
Christine Collins
Clarence Dupree
Cornelius Halliburton II
Danny Eve
Dupè Aleru
Elaine Hampton
Elizabeth Robinson
Erick Edwards
Gayle Schmidt
Greg Bowens
Jarita R. Halliburton
Jules Iles Sr.
K'Shanta R. Nunn
Keandra Stallworth
Kellie Halliburton
Ken Jones
Kent Wade
Kimberly Hambright-Brown
Kimberly Richardson
La'Shon Lake-Gardner
Laila Hanks
Linda Hunt
Lindell Johnson
Lisa Renee Halliburton
Lisa Yvette Jones

Lorri Carithers Lewis
Louis Hen Johnson Jr.
Mark Henfrey Smith
Michael Barham
Michelle Howard
Miesha Burton-Williams
Nanette Paine
Natasha Jackson
Pamela Hart
Precious Williams
Raja Wajahat Zahoor
Rhonda Wesley
Rosalyn Williams
Rose Marie Campbell
Sandra N. Peoples
Scherwin D. Halliburton
Selma Halliburton
Shawn A. Stephens
Sherene Levert
Sonya Davis
Stephanie L. H. Calahan
Stephanie Zackrie Avery
Sylvia Hubbard Hutula
Tamika L. Gaines
Tasha Sylvester
Tinisha Poitier
Tommy Johnson
Tonya Wells
Tracey Ilene
Trina Baker
Ty Parker
Unique LaCour
Val Ward

Dedication

This book is dedicated to all the powerful professional women with hidden potential who feel stuck in corporate America. I wrote this book to empower you to step out on faith, focus on your strengths, and monetize what you do best. Consider this book as a "sisterhood chat" that will prompt you to stop delaying your next level of greatness. By all means, you are women of excellence who have accomplished so much already; however, a more significant assignment is waiting for you. You've taken all the courses, attended all the webinars, showed up at all the conferences, and taken enough notes to have a best-selling book series with ten volumes!

I want to address the elephant in the room. It's time for you to stop hoping, waiting, and dreaming about launching your enterprise! The time is now! This is the sign for which you've been waiting! You already know that you're the best at what you do. Let's go! It's implementation time, ladies! Put a price tag on your expertise, provide excellence to your tribe, and *skyrocket your success*!

Cheers to your success!

Queashar L. Halliburton

Introduction

Welcome to *Skyrocket Your Success 2.0: The Corporate Women's Road Map to Navigate from Employee to Entrepreneur! Skyrocket Your Success 2.0* helps professional women stuck in corporate America impede self-sabotaging behaviors, use their skills to monetize their genius, and create a blueprint for optimal success in life and entrepreneurship.

Skyrocket Your Success 2.0 will empower you to honor your genius while acknowledging that you belong in the marketplace as a business owner. The strategies taught in this book will help you diffuse self-doubt, boost your confidence, and develop a champion mindset necessary for success!

After reading this book, I hope you'll feel that spark of inspiration to start making strides toward your next level of greatness—entrepreneurship. Your future clients are waiting on *you* to solve *their* problems. They've suffered in silence long enough. They've prayed, hoped, and wished for someone like you to provide much-needed solutions.

Years ago, my friend captured a photo of me shooting pool at a coworker's 50th birthday party. The photo recently appeared in my Facebook memories, and I had an instant epiphany about the game of pool. I pondered the meaning of the game of pool and came up with this revelation. The pool table represents life, and the balls represent opportunities in life.

The objective of the game of pool is to pot all eight balls. If we don't plan our next move, we can't pot the balls (or achieve our goals in life.) Successfully making shots, or potting the balls, in one of the corner pockets represents the success we can actualize when we strategize and take a shot by utilizing our God-given gifts to skyrocket our success.

Life has given me multiple opportunities to obtain career satisfaction. I'd tried about every career in which I was interested—public relations, teaching, auto sales, insurance, and real estate, and construction management; yet, something was *still missing*. Within each discipline, I did my best and obtained excellent skills that have allowed me great learning opportunities. After each trial and error, the insurance gig stuck; and now, I've made a living as an insurance agent for over two decades.

Despite having all these wonderful career experiences, I still was I operating within the confines of my comfort zone. I allowed fear to stop me from pursuing what I genuinely wanted. I wanted more freedom and flexibility within my career. I wanted to help women achieve their greatest potential in life. I got tired of being safe. I was getting older, and my hair was getting grayer. I was determined to level up and start accomplishing my personal entrepreneurial goals. Fed up with being bound by "safety," I took that leap into entrepreneurship and followed my dreams of becoming an author, speaker, and success coach. That picture I described is a constant reminder to *take your best shot and soar*!

Don't let the fear of failure, perfectionism, and the imposter syndrome stop you from doing what you are called to do. I want to encourage professional women who are millennials and Generation X to disallow the fear of failure that keeps you waiting on the sidelines. Just get started and follow your dreams today. Not living to your full potential is tragic, especially if your procrastination hinders another person's productivity. We all have God-given gifts that were meant to bless others and help them achieve greatness; but if we don't do what we are called to do, we can stunt the growth and potential of ourselves *and* others. Accept your calling and operate in excellence.

The *Skyrocket Your Success* series was created with *you* in mind. As a personal development coaching tool, this series will empower you to stop procrastinating, eliminate self-sabotaging behaviors, and monetize your gifts today. Elevate your mindset and stop second-guessing your abilities. You are good enough because God already has blessed you with everything you need to succeed! The time is now! Stop procrastinating and activate your dream of entrepreneurship.

This book introduces my four-part framework called the A.R.B.A. Methodology™. The following four steps will empower you to dominate in entrepreneurship:

Assess & Discover Your Zone of Genius!

Remove Obstacles & Develop a Champion Mindset!

Build Your Business and Skyrocket Your Success!

Activate, Maintain, and Sustain Your Enterprise!

Here is a brief explanation of my methodology.

PHASE #1

Assess & Discover Your Zone of Genius!

Assess where you are and imagine where you want to be in your career. Acknowledge that you are unfulfilled in your career because you know you are meant to be an entrepreneur. Tally your current skill set and consider your value. Discover your specialty and create a plan to monetize and package your unique brilliance.

PHASE #2

Remove Obstacles & Develop a Champion Mindset!

Redefine your definition of success and develop a champion mindset for entrepreneurship. This can be achieved by identifying and removing all self-sabotaging hindrances that keep your gifts hidden. You must abolish the fixed, self-defeating mindset and nurture a winning growth mindset that will allow you to overcome the obstacles and setbacks with your next phase.

PHASE #3

Build Your Business and Skyrocket Your Success!

Build and legally establish a recession-proof enterprise based on your valuable skills. Get locked in with a coach/mentor to skyrocket your growth. Develop your strategic plan that focuses on your specialty. Collaborate and build a dream team of experts to skyrocket your business.

PHASE #4

Activate, Maintain, and Sustain Your Enterprise!

Activate your God-given gifts and reign in entrepreneurship. Create and cultivate a great company culture that will facilitate the preservation of your business, build a legacy, and create generational wealth. The organizational culture embodies a company's shared beliefs, values, and goals, and it also guides the organization's behavior. Make sure your goals and values align with the needs of your core team and employees. You must be open to employee feedback, enabling you to grow and pivot based on your organization's needs.

Imagine how your life would change for the best only if you stopped overthinking things and just went for it? How fulfilled would your life be if you just took that shot? Think about how many lives you can impact positively only if you just operate in your purpose. Remember that you are unstoppable! You've got this! I'm rooting for you, my sister! Start your transformation today.

Chapter One

Being Stuck Is No Longer An Excuse!

"It's never too late to follow your dreams."

Are you a professional woman who feels stuck in corporate America? You are achieving great strides in your personal life and professional career. You have accomplished a lot by most standards, and you have climbed the corporate ladder of success. Pat yourself on the back and celebrate yourself for achieving success in your career.

Despite many of the successes you have accomplished in your career, somehow, you still feel empty in the pit of your belly like something is *missing*. The missing link is that you are not operating in your whole purpose. Sometimes, we put our goals and dreams on the back-burner because we are caught up in or hypnotized by our "9 to 5." Sadly, this hypnosis keeps us stuck in our everyday routine. Being stuck evokes unenthusiasm, a lack of motivation, stagnation, and it may even sap your creativity.

Fear has blocked you from pursuing your dream of entrepreneurship. You are ignoring the gifts God has placed inside you, and your gifts and talents lie dormant. Not knowing how to begin your entrepreneurship is no longer an excuse. You must take charge of your life and career. Don't let fear and life's challenges be your excuses for remaining stuck. Get out of that rut, girl! Be strategic about pursuing your entrepreneurial goals.

Living in your purpose means fully operating in the calling that God has placed inside every individual. It's that one place where you shine. It's what you're called to do in life. If you are multitalented like me, this journey can get confusing. God gives each of us an assignment in life; however, we don't always operate in our purpose because we are trapped in our everyday routines and careers. Operating in your true purpose takes self-discovery, time, commitment, prayer, and action.

Don't put your gifts on the back-burner. It's never too late to reach your full potential and achieve your wildest dreams. Many of us don't accomplish our dreams because *fear* prevents us from even trying. Imagining that our goals are unreachable causes many of us to get stuck. If we put our goals in writing and work towards them a little each day, our goals will become attainable. If we feed into negative thinking, then our goals become unreachable. Every time we feed the negative thoughts, our goals become insurmountable, and we trick ourselves into thinking we can't achieve them. However, let me tell you something; if there is breath in your lungs, there is still time to pursue your life's dreams and goals.

The first step to pursue your dream starts with acknowledging where you are and where you want to be. This first step includes being honest with yourself and admitting you're not in alignment with your purpose. If you're not doing the thing you dream about doing, and you are not working in your zone of genius, then you're just existing. You must decide what you want to do and create a plan to start working on it and operating within your God-given purpose. Feeling stuck in life is a terrible feeling.

After trying out every available career, I eventually found my niche as a licensed insurance agent. After decades of working as an insurance agent, I felt an inner push to do more. Writing used to be essential to my life, and I discovered that I actually missed it. Since elementary school, one of my lifelong dreams was to become an author. Writing was customary for me throughout my entire school career—from elementary school through college. I used to write poetry, and I participated in writing contests. Eventually, I became a writer for the school newspaper. I entered college as a communications major at Michigan State University; however, when I graduated, I leaped into the corporate arena. As a result, my writing took a back seat. I often would pick up a pen and a notebook, and I would plan to write a book; however, I would never complete what I started. After decades of procrastinating, that deep desire to fulfill my dream of authoring a book reemerged. Despite having deep urges to write, I refused to do it. It became an inner battle.

"I will do it later," I told myself repeatedly. It wasn't long before the fear of failure set in. I didn't know if my writing would be "good enough" for a book that someone actually would want to read. My procrastination got so bad that I had trouble sleeping at night. Despite these obstacles, I kept feeling a push to author a book. In 2008, I started writing my first novel, but then I got to chapter eight. I called it, "The Chapter 8 Blues." Then, procrastination made its grand reentrance, and I put my book on ice.

I was determined to return to my book later, but I never returned to writing it. I tangoed with procrastination until 2017. I got tired and switched dance partners. I dumped procrastination and started writing a blog about being productive and overcoming success blockers. This blog not only helped me to start writing again, but also it provided the fuel I needed to accomplish my dream of finally becoming an author. I used the content from my blog and wrote my first eBook entitled, *Everything They Won't Tell You About Procrastination*. I was able to present at a few workshops with this eBook. In the future, I aim to offer these workshops in the corporate arena and at women's conferences.

Because of that one eBook, my life has changed for the better! That book was the springboard that launched me into my purpose as an *authorpreneur* (an author and entrepreneur). Becoming an author has allowed me to connect with people worldwide, including being under the tutelage of the world's best motivational speaker, Mr. Les Brown. My story illustrates the principle of strategically pursuing your purpose. It will not happen magically; you must take action to pursue the entrepreneurial goals and dreams that lie dormant inside you. Once you get past all the excuses, procrastination, and even the "imposter syndrome," taking action will lead to a more fulfilled life and give you the platform to empower others to achieve greatness. I know I'm fulfilling my purpose, and I'm ready to elevate to the next level.

Being stuck is no longer an excuse! Consider the following five helpful strategies to become unstuck while transitioning into your next level of entrepreneurship.

1. Specify what goals you want to accomplish. Grab a journal and label it, "Business Journal." Use this journal to brainstorm all your business ideas. Create a checklist for each activity and mark each task as complete when done.

2. Take inventory of your time to learn when you have free time within your schedule to work solely on your business ideas. Schedule and dedicate at least one hour a day to

work on your projects. Set reminders on your phone by using an alarm. *Do not ignore this alarm.* Select the best time of day to work on your business goals. If dedicating one hour is impossible, you can schedule two separate, thirty-minute sessions each day if necessary.

3. Identify any obstacles that may hinder you from achieving your goals. Write down each issue along with a solution to overcome that challenge. Taking the initiative to solve potential problems before they even occur will halt any hindrances that may delay you from accomplishing your business goals.

4. Educate yourself more about your specialty and the entrepreneurship journey. Research what people are being paid in your area of expertise. Brainstorm and identify areas where you can provide more value than competitors. Research and find out where your competitors may lack proficiency. This will be an area where you can focus on, learn about, and dominate in your area of expertise. Google and YouTube can be extremely helpful research tools; just make sure you're gaining information from reputable sources.

5. Connect with business professionals who are highly successful in your area of expertise. Use LinkedIn, professional organizations, and business groups on social media to connect with and learn from superstar entrepreneurs who work in your specialty.

CHAPTER ONE CHECKPOINT:

1. Have you pursued your dream of entrepreneurship? If not, why haven't you?

_____

_____

_____

_____

2. Describe your first entry in your new business journal.

_____

_____

_____

_____

3. What is your area of expertise?

_____

_____

_____

_____

Chapter Two

Tap Into Your Zone Of Genius!

"Flip your side-hustle into a profitable woman-owned enterprise!"

I magine being caught up in the rat race in corporate America. You feel like it's time for a shift, but you just ignore that urgency to elevate to your next level of greatness. You know your job like the back of your hand. You can perform your work activities so well that you can do some work tasks in your sleep. There was a time in my two decades as an insurance agent when I felt invisible in the workplace. I wasn't interested in moving to another department, but I knew it was time for a *shift*. I felt misaligned deep down inside because *purpose* was growing inside me.

I felt a push to do more; I had to answer the call to *purpose*. Deep within, I felt an urgency to pursue some entrepreneurial goals like speaking professionally and hosting workshops and conferences to empower women; however, I just ignored it. I allowed life and work to get in the way of my true calling and love for writing. After early career disappointments, I put my entrepreneurial goals on hold and regretted it.

After some deep soul-searching, intense prayer, and personal development, I pushed myself to do the thing I had been avoiding. That very thing started with writing. I felt an inner peace whenever I picked up a pen and a notebook. I was doing what I was meant to do—communicating through written words, so I could shift the mindset of women who also were meant to do more. I know that God has blessed me with the gift of empowering women to use their innate abilities to stop waiting on the sidelines, take control of their futures, and build a legacy.

Identifying our superpowers can be a personal struggle that may cause conflict within. No one knows you better than yourself, right? I believe that we each have a true calling in this life. When God created each of us, He had a purpose in mind. It may take decades to discover your unique genius because we use it daily. Your unique genius may be just part of your daily routine; meanwhile, others see it as a gift. It's not evident to us because it's not a gift in our own eyes; it's just a part of us. If there is any confusion when identifying your purpose in life, I implore you to pray and ask God to reaffirm your purpose.

As women of purpose, we go through multiple seasons in life. If you are a believer, you may be familiar with the passage of Scripture that talks about seasons. Ecclesiastes 3:1-2 NLT says, "For everything, there is a season, a time for every activity under heaven. A time to be born and a time to die. A time to plant and a time to harvest."[1] Sometimes, we are in the middle of a season of change; therefore, we must first gain clarity and know the season in which we find ourselves. When you are in tune with God, He will confirm your purpose and let you reap the harvest of the seeds you've sown through your work and dedication throughout your career.

We also must be in tune with self-sabotaging behaviors that delay us from reaching our fullest potential in life. We must be honest and call out the hindrances that keep us from achieving our goals and dreams. Take the initiative and write out a list of your top three hindrances. After reviewing your list, you immediately can produce solutions to address your top three concerns. You also can discuss these potential issues with a mentor or a mental health professional to gain more insight and guidance regarding ways to address your self-sabotaging behaviors.

The *imposter syndrome* makes you feel like you are not good enough to have a seat at the table. The inferiority

---

[1] See References.

complex may be a symptom of something from your past that has not been addressed. Most times, this feeling may stem from something from your childhood. It may have been something negative that someone you cared about said to you when you were a little girl. The negativity experienced from a previous situation planted a seed of doubt, and you watered it, nurtured it, and gave it some sunlight. Now, that seed of doubt has grown into a tree of procrastination.

This syndrome causes you to get caught up in the comparison game. It's easy to get caught in this trap, especially when you log into your favorite social media platform where overnight success reigns supreme. On social media, it seems as if so many social media influencers have ridden the escalator to success, while most people have to climb the ladder of success. Sometimes, it can seem unreachable for the average professional who has been putting in the work for years without a glimpse of success. The imposter syndrome causes you to second guess your ability. It makes you feel like you are doing something wrong. It can cause you to mimic what others are doing and veer off your journey to success.

We must recognize that our journey to success will be unique. Although someone may influence your journey, we must not get consumed in comparing ourselves to others. Focusing on someone else's journey can deter you from being your authentic self. You must remain genuine and honest about your challenges and setbacks. These difficulties help us become more resilient and teach us how to deal with life's unexpected twists and turns. We must achieve victory by following the distinctive path set before us based on our unique life experiences. Know that you are good enough. With dedication, mentorship, and education, you will make it to the top.

God has blessed us with unique abilities, so we can build generational wealth. Whether we know it or not, we are all experts. We need to identify where we shine and create a plan to monetize our skills in the marketplace. Many may be challenged with identifying their gifts and expertise. Thinking about what people love about us is an effortless way to start. What are a few things that people compliment you on? Think about all the extraordinary gifts and skills that bring happiness to your family, friends, and the community. You even can consider some things you are often asked to do.

For instance, when you are at work and have a particular project, does your name often come up when a supervisor or team leader asks for a volunteer? Do you have excellent leadership skills? Are you a great organizer? Do you have excellent people skills? Do you work well under pressure? Are you a great collaborator? These are things to consider while analyzing your gifts and strengths.

Assess Your Skill Set and Discover Your Zone of Genius

Let's do a quick assessment to help identify your zone of genius.

Take a personal inventory of your skills. Ask your family, friends, and business associates to tell you what you're good at doing. If you are having difficulty getting started, look at your resume. Do you have letters of recommendation from colleagues? After reviewing responses from your tribe, do you notice any recurring skills or talents? Do you see a pattern of the same things mentioned? Also, think about your volunteer positions and assess what you've done professionally, personally, or socially. What have you contributed to family functions? Are you the one who organizes your family reunions, meetings, or holiday functions? List all your awards, kudos, or reviews that you have received in the past five years. Ask business associates, mentors, coaches, and accountability partners for their input. Jot everything down. Get on your social media platforms and ask questions. Once you gather all your info, read and review your list. Look for a common theme.

Create a top-five list and use a scale from 1-5. Five should be the thing that gives you the slightest joy, and 1 should be the thing that brings you the most joy. Remember that the number one position you select must be something you enjoy and can monetize from.

Once you have your list in place, go to Google to research careers or entrepreneurial endeavors you can pursue that align with your top skills.

Research top coaches and mentors in your area of expertise. Do your homework and find out everything you can about the coaches. Visit their social media profiles, follow them, and consume their free content. If their content is helpful to you in accomplishing an immediate goal, then contact them and thank them. Build a relationship with coaches who resonate with you. You can start by liking and commenting on their social media posts. Then, you can narrow down your list to your top three. See if you can set up a discovery call to see if you are a good fit to collaborate with them.

Write out a success plan. Envision what success looks like for you if you achieved your wildest dreams. Create a legacy based on your expertise. Journal about it, pray about it, and then create a plan to make it your reality.

CHAPTER TWO CHECKPOINT:

1. Discuss a time when you felt misaligned in the workplace and felt that you should be doing something more suited to your life's purpose. How did you manage the feeling of unfulfillment at your 9 to 5?

_____

_____

_____

_____

2. Name two recession-proof skills from which you can monetize.

_____

_____

_____

_____

3. If you can imagine succeeding as a woman-led enterprise, what would be your biggest challenge with getting started?

_____

_____

_____

_____

Chapter Three

Elevate Your Mindset For Entrepreneurship!

"You have earned a seat at the table!"

The roller coaster of emotions experienced during the beginning phases of your entrepreneurial journey can sometimes leave you feeling depleted and longing for an emotional retreat. You must develop a growth mindset to help you overcome self-sabotaging and unforeseen obstacles that can derail your progress in your transition to entrepreneurship.

Those with a fixed mindset usually have difficulty handling life situations and circumstances because they are limited in their belief system, and they are not open to change and growth. They believe that their skills and abilities are fixed. A growth mindset will enable you to nurture your current skills and abilities through training, coaching, and implementing what you have learned. You also will understand that your success will be limitless if you continue to hone your craft and keep learning through personal development.

I admit that I was dealing with imposter syndrome early on in my publishing business. I had the education, experience, training, and ability, but I procrastinated because I thought everything had to be perfect before I could leap into my calling.

I refused to start taking clients because there was always something more I needed to know before I started coaching clients. I kept going in the cycle of taking many courses, workshops, and webinars, and trying to soak in everything. I highly consumed so much information with no implementation of what I learned.

I was overly consumed with so much knowledge that it was hard for me to rest sometimes. There were times when I fell asleep while listening to webinars. It got crazy and became an obsession. I was overthinking it all, and I felt like I was going to fail. Consequently, my lack of implementation caused me to miss a lot of money. I would meet with clients and find a reason to refer them to other publishers. I felt overwhelmed and ill-prepared to manage everything necessary to run my business.

I had to do a lot of personal development work like reading, coaching, praying, and mindset work. I also had to reaffirm myself and build my confidence by putting all the knowledge I learned into action. Constant personal development is fundamental during the growing stages of entrepreneurship. Seeking personal development and implementing what you learned will help elevate your confidence. You are investing in your growth while increasing your business acumen.

Personal development coaching and training allow you to elevate your mindset because you broaden your perspective and gain more clarity on infinite possibilities for continued growth. Tapping into resources like mentorship and establishing a team of successful entrepreneurial friends will help keep you grounded and accountable. Building these relationships will help you get through the rough patches of business.

As surely as the wind blows, there always will be days when you feel invincible, like you can do anything. Then, there will be days when you feel emotionally depleted and need a place to retreat to mentally. How does one deal with the constant rejection and other disappointments in the beginning stages of entrepreneurship?

The first key to build a champion mindset is establishing boundaries. Establishing boundaries can help increase your productivity and provide a sense of retreat as you blossom into the successful business person you are called to be. Here are some quick ways to set up a few healthy boundaries. It can be as simple as setting up a specific time to answer calls or return emails. Make sure that you are managing clients by appointment only or setting up discovery calls to ensure the customer is a good fit for your business. Finally, make sure that you have at least one day per week to *unplug* and *rest*.

Another important way to elevate your entrepreneurship mindset is to prioritize quality self-care. Setting up a healthy routine will empower you to maintain your normalcy. Whatever you do, choose something that will build you emotionally, physically, and spiritually.

Quality self-care can include:

- Spending time with your family and friends.
- Getting a monthly massage.
- Praying
- Reading books within your favorite genre.
- Taking a walk.
- Unplugging from your everyday routine.

INCREASE YOUR EMOTIONAL INTELLIGENCE AS YOU PREPARE FOR ENTREPRENEURSHIP

According to the Oxford English Dictionary, emotional intelligence is often defined as "the ability to understand your emotions and those of other people and to behave in an appropriate way in different situations."[2] Identifying your emotional triggers is most helpful. You must be able to recognize when your emotions are getting the best of you, and you must identify when your emotional well-being is not in alignment.

You must be able to acknowledge when your feelings are preventing you from making sound decisions. We've all had days when we don't feel like ourselves. Think about a time when you were not making great choices, and you felt it in your gut. Your intuition is leading you one way, but you make the opposite choice that is not based on the direction in which you need to be headed.

The following is a three-part process that will help you determine if your feelings are unbalanced. It also may help you realize if you have unresolved issues that must be addressed. Consider if the following suggestions can help you become more aware of your emotions and help you determine if you need to talk to someone to get help addressing your emotional needs. You will be able to identify where you need more healing and validation. You can start

---

[2] See References.

journaling and decide if you want to talk to someone to help resolve your issues.

Self-management is key. Here are three ways that you immediately can begin to manage your emotions: **E.R.D.** – Evaluate, Recall, and Deal™.

1. **Evaluate** your situation. Be honest with yourself. Are your emotions out of control? Do you feel like there is an imbalance in your behavior or feelings? If so, don't ignore your feelings. Immediately acknowledge your feelings and take a mental note of your behavior.

2. **Recall** how you have been reacting to recent stressful situations. Have you been avoiding them altogether? Avoidance seems like a quick fix, but ignoring your issues will cause them to resurface if they are not addressed.

3. **Deal** with the situation when it happens. Please don't put it off. Feel the emotions. Deal with the situation and talk about them with a trusted person immediately. This way, you will not lose sleep over it. Manage the issue right away.

Sometimes, it may be hard to self-manage your emotions; that's why you always should have a backup plan. Your backup plan should include talking with a trusted family member or accountability partner. Most importantly, reach out for professional help by speaking with a mental health counselor, if necessary. Help is available twenty-four hours a day, seven days a week. Try an online site like betterhealth.com.

BUILDING A CHAMPION MINDSET FOR ENTREPRENEURSHIP

Building a champion mindset is one of the essential elements when transitioning to entrepreneurship. Self-confidence in your skills will get you to the next level. You must know that what you offer to this world is beneficial. Your expertise is valuable, and people need what you offer to change their lives and move them forward in accomplishing their own life goals and vision.

Our feelings are sometimes just temporary; therefore, we should not let how we feel today stop us from moving forward in our business endeavors. When planning your business, it's essential to have your plans in writing. You should schedule a time to work on your business daily, whether you feel motivated or not. Don't let your temporary emotions determine if you will or will not take action on your dream. Make a list of 100 things you need to do for your business and do one thing daily. That way, if you are having an emotional day, you have a prepared list to work through.

I've experienced days when I felt like just admitting defeat. Then, the next day, the next level. Therefore, it's normal to have those feelings, but you must push through and do what's necessary to move forward in life and business. Give yourself grace and rest to replenish your strength when necessary. To avoid burnout, take your time to rest. Once you're rejuvenated, then you can get back to work.

Let's consider three emotional mindset stages of the burgeoning entrepreneur: The first stage is the *Tyro Mindset*; the second stage is the *Collaborative Mindset*, and the final stage is the *Champion Mindset*. Each stage provides development and a learning curve for the ambitious entrepreneur.

Stage 1: The Tyro Mindset. During this initial mindset stage, novice entrepreneurs are open to new possibilities. They are unbiased due to inexperience, and they make decisions based upon present situations and circumstances. Fresh eyes perpetuate a fresh perspective. In this emotional mindset stage, business owners have an open mind and are inquisitive as they mark their territory in the marketplace. They value the importance of learning something new. The "Imposter Syndrome" sometimes can paralyze them with procrastination and doubts concerning their ability to accomplish the goals and dreams that God has placed inside them. They immerse themselves in their new business by gaining more knowledge through mentorship, coaching, reading, and practicing their craft. Confidence builds as the entrepreneurs gain more experience and knowledge in their niche. Networking with other entrepreneurs will be essential during this stage. Self-actualization becomes evident during this stage. The individuals are becoming fully aware of their valuable skills and the ways to use them to create wealth.

The business professionals gain more insight and realize their growth potential.

Stage 2: Collaborative Mindset. This mindset stage focuses on looking at the bigger picture. Within this stage, you'll see how the business enterprise can benefit from specialized skills within the organization and outside partnerships. Finding partners with complementary skill sets can help build a strong dream team. Transparency, honesty, and effective communication are essential for a constructive and collaborative relationship. During this emotional mindset stage, the collaborative framework of the business is solidified. The unity displayed amongst the team facilitates a solid partnership. The realization that no one can build alone exists, and the business owner encourages his partners to align for the greater good. Working in your zone of genius is emphasized because it strengthens partnerships and focuses on professionals mastering their complementary area of expertise.

Stage 3: The Champion Mindset. At this point in the entrepreneurial growth stage, business professionals are proficient in their expertise. Experience guides the process, which has been mastered through multiple years of success within their niche. The entrepreneurs are resolute in decision-making, and they are systematic with every move. Judgment is based on historical information and past experiences. The entrepreneurs know their businesses, understand current market conditions, and recognize how the market responds to them. They take initiative with high emotional intelligence because they have overcome multiple challenges while operating their enterprise. Professional businesses display a strong will to succeed and understand that competition makes them stronger and more resourceful. They set realistic goals and accomplish them with ease. They have built a solid relationship with their target market and provide valuable solutions to their clients.

As previously discussed, being in control of your emotions is crucial to balance your energy level and productivity daily. Ongoing commitment to personal development is essential to maintain a positive state of mind and emotional stability. Building your emotional intelligence and being clear about how you can best serve your clients are key to building a sustainable business and the ever-changing global economy.

Here are a few ways to lean into your strengths as you build your confidence and elevate a champion mindset for entrepreneurship.

1. Release the idea that everything has to be perfect *before* you leap into entrepreneurship. Everything won't be perfect; start where you are. As you take action, everything will eventually fall into place. Don't be afraid to ask for help. Operate in your expertise and delegate other tasks to your team or contractors when necessary.

2. Reaffirm your qualifications by taking an accurate inventory of your accomplishments. List ten things you have accomplished professionally and personally within

the past five years. Update your resume and then combine your achievements into a brag book. A brag book is like a personal scrapbook with a compilation of your achievements or anything that makes you feel proud. It's different from a business journal, which is where you write about your business goals. The brag book is a physical photobook in which you can place pictures and documents that honor your achievements. You will have physical proof of the wonderful things that you have accomplished. You also can create a brag wall where you can display photos of your accomplishments. I created a brag wall using Mixtiles where I took photos and turned them into framed wall art.

You can include pictures of your family and friends, awards, acknowledgements, kudos from co-workers or associates, testimonials, or certificates. When you are having a dreadful day and feel like you are not good enough, open your brag book! View your accomplishments and bask in your greatness! Doing this activity will empower you to acknowledge your greatness!

3. Get rid of the negative mindset. Retrain your brain to think positively. Do daily exercises to reverse your negative thinking. Just like you train for a marathon, you must retrain your brain intentionally to think positively! It is a discipline that's mastered only through consistent practice. Try this exercise to retrain your brain. When a negative thought that makes you feel unworthy, envision

that you are the picture of success. Envision yourself winning! Say positive affirmations that build you up. Know that you are worthy of all the success you desire in this lifetime.

CHAPTER THREE CHECKPOINT:

1. Do you have a fixed mindset or a growth mindset?

_____

_____

_____

_____

2. Do you feel like you're being attacked when someone gives you suggestions that will help take your career to the next level? Being open to feedback from a mentor or coach can help you achieve previously unattainable goals.

_____

_____

_____

_____

3. What are some of the accomplishments that you will share in your brag book?

_____

_____

_____

_____

Chapter Four

Redefine Your Success Journey!

"Bask in the limelight of your success!"

In my modern-day study entitled, ***"The Success Factor Survey,"*** [3] which was conducted in the fall of 2017, 66% of respondents said that they felt successful. Defining one's success is an arbitrary notion. Once you've experienced the difficulties of life and business, you become familiar with what life has to offer. Based on your goals, you'll rediscover what's important and impactful in your life. This realization causes you to re-evaluate things and develop new goals and ideas for success.

---

[3] Please see "The Success Factor Study Results" at the end of Chapter 4.

Redefining success means redetermining what makes you happy and fulfilled in your career and in your personal life based on your current situation. After failing to maintain a career in the communications industry, I had to pivot and learn a new profession. In my new career as an insurance agent, I defined success through personal achievement, the respect I gained from others, and my influence. Although money is always necessary, it was not my dominating reason for working hard. I was never obsessed with becoming rich because I knew that if I worked hard and set goals, I eventually would make the money I desired. Making a positive impact on the lives of others excited me. I desired to help to make life easier for others.

When I began my career, I remember seeing "Agent of the Year" plaques scattered on the walls. I knew that one day, the agency would post my photo amongst the ranks of the best-selling insurance agents. As I matured in my career journey, I began to value flexibility and freedom in my everyday life. Growing up, I was taught that I would be successful if I earned a college degree and found an excellent job in my preferred field of study. Later, I discovered that this route to success is not necessarily the golden ticket for everyone. As your career path blossoms, you have unique needs at various levels in your career.

You must recalibrate and determine what success means to you at each stage in your career. You must be self-aware and evaluate your life based on your personal interpretation of success. Consider what represents success for you based on your own goals. What makes you feel accomplished? You must reject external factors that subliminally dominate your definition of success. Success often is determined by our own past experiences, victories, and failures. We must evaluate what we've learned and reposition ourselves based on our new personal missions and purpose.

When you redefine success, you can envision and create the life that you are meant to live. You can raise your expectations and create a higher standard of living for yourself and your family. Creating new boundaries will allow you to shift your way of thinking. This will introduce you to a new perspective, expectations, and a new level of achievement. These changes will allow you to live your life on your terms, which also will empower you to stop living for others and will cause you to lean into your abilities and life desires.

When redefining success, we should revisit our past failures and use these as stepping stones to our future success. The beauty behind failure is that it provides a space for us to rethink the process and experiment with new possibilities. These encounters show us what doesn't work and teach us life lessons that help us to navigate life and make wiser decisions. Failure strengthens us and helps us lean into our skills and abilities. Sometimes, failure causes us to ask for help. It makes us accountable for learning from our mistakes, trying new possibilities, becoming creative, and seeking a new process to solve a problem.

Throughout life, we go through distinct phases, and what's important to us changes. We must consider the stage in which we find ourselves and create a new way of doing things. **Here are a few ways to pivot, create new expectations, and redefine your success.**

1. The first step is to acknowledge that you are in a new season of your life and career. New seasons require a shift in your mindset and a change in your environment. You must re-evaluate your surroundings and create a clutter-free space to discover your new level.

2. Be clear about what you desire in life and put it in writing. Journal about your perfect day. Take note of how you want your day to flow. Take note of how you feel. How does your environment look? Who is in your network of support? Be descriptive about your expectations. *Design the life that you want.*

3. Check your circle. Everyone in your circle should be adding value to your life, not depleting your life. Remove anyone who is not adding value to your life.

4. Make a weekly, monthly, quarterly, and annual top five list of things that you want to accomplish for the year. Have an accountability partner check in monthly to monitor your progress. If something does not feel right, permit yourself to change it. Give yourself grace.

5. Celebrate each success every step of the way. Celebrating your success will solidify your

accomplishments and empower you to create a new definition of success on your own terms.

We all define success differently. Distinct factors make us feel accomplished in life and our careers. When I was researching for this book, I tapped Facebook friends and asked them to provide powerful words that affirmed success for them. This survey was completed September 6, 2020.

HERE IS THE LIST OF SUCCESS-AFFIRMING WORDS BELOW:

Abundance, accomplished, accomplishment, accountability, ambition, best, better, Black Panther Movement, blessings, born-again, challenging work, choices, college education, comfort, commitment, confident, consistency, contentment, courage, dedication, delegation, determination, discipline, distinguished, dreams, driven, education, effort, emotional intelligence, empowered, endurance, ethic, evaluation, execution, failure, faith, family, focus, freedom, generational wealth, purposeful, God, good health, gratitude, growth, happiness, hardworking, healing, health, homeowner, humility, impact, investment, Jesus, journey, joy, knowledge, leadership, legacy, listen, love, loyalty, meaning, money, more, motivation, passion, patience, peace, peace of mind, perseverance, plans, power, prayer, prosperity, purpose, quality friendships, read, relentless, resilience, resources, respect, responsibility, sacrifice, security, self-sufficient, service, solace, stability, strength, struggle, successful children, the-next-generation, to help others, undeniable, wealth, work.

THE SUCCESS FACTOR SURVEY RESULTS

Q1 What is your definition of success?

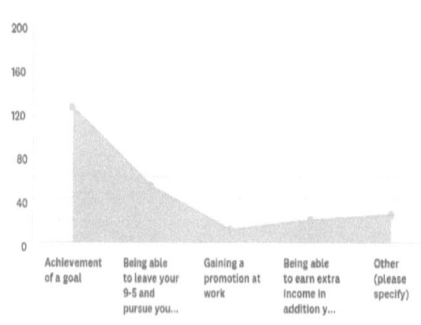

Q2 Do you feel like you are successful?

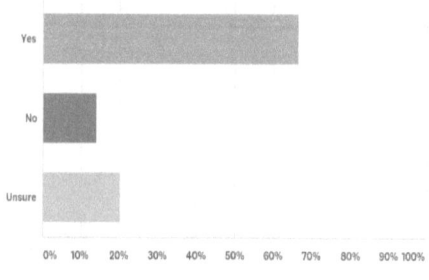

Q3 Do you feel anxious about your success?

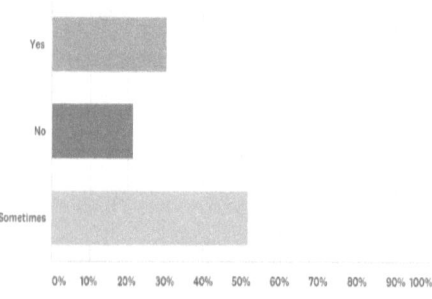

Q4 What factors affect your success?

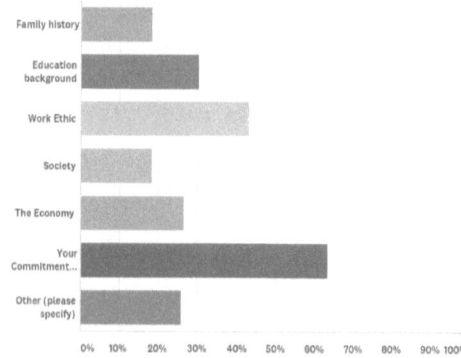

Q5 What is the one thing holding you back from becoming successful in life?

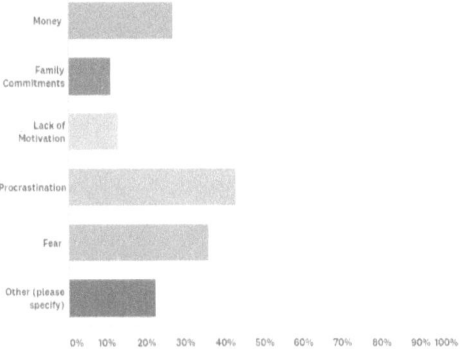

Q6 How do you maintain success?

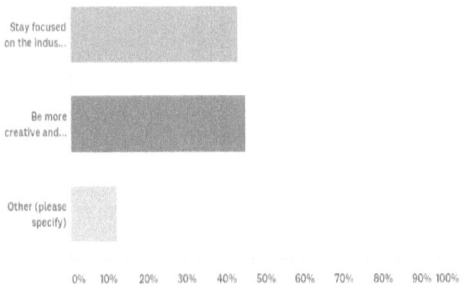

CHAPTER FOUR CHECKPOINT:

1. Share a few ways your definition of success has changed as you have matured.

_____

_____

_____

_____

2. How has failure helped you redetermine your definition of success?

_____

_____

_____

_____

3. What are three things that are non-negotiable on your journey to entrepreneurship?

_____

_____

_____

_____

Chapter Five

Incorporate, Build & Collaborate!

"Be authentically you! Embrace your "It"
Factor!"

Congratulations on your progress thus far! You have acknowledged and assessed your skill set, identified your zone of genius, identified potential obstacles that may hinder you from achieving entrepreneurial goals, and suggested a solution to avoid detours. You have also nurtured and developed a champion mindset for successful entrepreneurship. It's time to level up and prepare for the entrepreneurship journey.

During the beginning stages of my entrepreneurship journey, I was in the process of publishing my first book. A publishing mentor convinced me to establish a publishing company, so I could self-publish. I didn't know where to start. I did not know how to establish my business name, so I contacted Legal Zoom to assist me with beginning the incorporation process and obtaining my tax identification number. Establishing a publishing company was never in my plans, so I had no idea what I should name my business. My coach suggested I name my publishing company, "Shardetroit Publishing." Unfortunately, that name was unavailable; so I used my first name to create the business name and decided on the title, Queashar Detroit Publishing, LLC. Later, I learned how to apply independently for an LLC and tax identification number.

After applying for my LLC and EIN, I opened a bank account and applied for a credit card under my business name. I also started researching liability insurance rates for a business owner's policy. When I first established my business, I had no plans to offer publishing services; it was just a way to self-publish my book and other family members' books. I didn't publish my first book until a year later because I had too much going on that year. My time was minimal. I worked full-time as an insurance agent and went to graduate school, and I was chairperson for an upcoming scholarship gala.

During the first year I established my business, I created a survey research study for my upcoming book on success. It was called, "The Success Factor." I sought out people's views on success and asked them to tell me what was hindering them from becoming successful in life. This research later became the foundation of my *Skyrocket Your Success* book series.

I also established a social media presence and documented my journey to become a published author. Creating a social media page and documenting my progress in real time kept me accountable as I completed my first book. Although I had established a publishing business, I had no idea how to monetize it strategically. I hired a coach who advised me to start taking clients and help them publish their books. I wasn't ready to start taking clients because I didn't have my own book published, and I didn't have any processes or systems set up for clients.

I felt lost and stuck in the process because I had not intended to start a publishing company. I just wanted to write and hold off on offering publishing services until I had a few systems in place. After doing research and learning about the routes to publishing, I determined that it was best for me to self-publish. I went ahead and established a publishing imprint, so I could publish my future books. I eventually published my first eBook in December 2018.

At the beginning of your journey, start connecting with other business owners within your niche to learn from them. You want to start networking and looking for successful potential mentors and coaches who specialize in your niche. I searched for local publishers with whom I could connect and learned from them concerning the publishing process. I found a local hybrid publishing company, *Claire Aldin Publications*. I connected with the company's president, Dr. De'Andrea Matthews, and became her coaching client.

Becoming Dr. Matthews' coaching client was one of the best decisions I made because she helped me establish a successful onboarding and publishing process for my clients. I have used the same process to date. Networking and building relationships with coaches and business professionals in your area of expertise is essential to become a successful entrepreneur. It's great to learn from those who already have accomplished success in their business and are willing to help you along the way.

Defining your expertise and the value you can provide to your customers is vital in business building. You must know that your expertise will solve a pain point for your target audience. Your business offering must be a needed service that you love and can monetize. Identify what product or service within your wheelhouse can be valuable to customers.

CRITICAL QUESTIONS TO ANSWER BEFORE ESTABLISHING YOUR BUSINESS

1. Are you an expert in your niche?
2. What product or service will you offer?
3. What is the business mission of your enterprise?

4. Who is your ideal customer?
5. Is there a demand for the services or products that you offer?
6. How will you finance your business?
7. Will your business be home-based, or will you have to secure a location?
8. Will you have employees or business contractors?

You must identify and research your top three to five competitors. Study your competitors. Do a SWOT analysis to discover a bird's eye view of a company's strengths, weaknesses, opportunities for growth, and threats within their business. Here is a brief description of the process that I learned in my strategic management course. A SWOT analysis is a strategic management tool that identifies internal strengths and weaknesses and external growth opportunities and threats that may cause harm to a business. The SWOT analysis aims to understand the company's current ability to compete in the marketplace. It allows one to see the company's proficient areas and areas in need of development, and they learn how to create a plan to improve aspects that need to be developed within the organization. Reviewing these options helps organizations identify their competencies and competitive advantage in the marketplace.

Here is a straightforward way to conduct a quick SWOT analysis to evaluate a few companies. First, select four companies that you would consider to be your main competition. Create a four-quadrant chart and label the top left quadrant S for Strengths and the top right quadrant W for Weaknesses. Label the lower left quadrant O for Opportunities and the lower right quadrant T for possible external Threats that may be a potential problem for the business. These threats are typically problems outside the organization's control.

Under each quadrant, list four to five items that correspond with each category. For instance, for Strengths, list the internal strengths of the company. Think about ways the company thrives and stands out amongst its competitors. What makes the company great? Does the company have a good reputation and a good presence in the community?

For Weaknesses, list four to five things that need improvement within the company. Think about where the company needs to improve. Are there any deficiencies on which the company needs to work? For instance, does the company need to have a faster process for responding to customer inquiries?

For Opportunities, ponder any external opportunities that can help the company further its mission. Are there any collaborations that can help the company accelerate growth in any of its goals?

Use the findings of your research to hone your business idea. Be sure to create a competitive edge by adding something that your competitors lacked. Use your research to help you create a viable business and marketing plan. If you are lost in creating a business plan, there are many organizations like SCORE and business coaches who can help you get started.

If you plan to build a *brand* and not just a business, consult with an intellectual property attorney before selecting your business name and entity. When you create your business name, you can run a search with your state in addition to the United States Patent and Trademark Office. Visit **uspto.gov** to see if the name is taken. Before you incorporate, you want to ensure that you are your business brand's owner.

Retaining an intellectual property attorney to conduct the trademark search for you would be ideal. This process will help ensure that another business does not own your desired business name and brand. I made this big mistake and didn't find out until years later. I created a podcast based on the name of one of my books, and I later found out that I couldn't trademark the name of my podcast because another podcast had a similar name. Keeping that name could cause brand confusion in a similar market. Learning this fundamental lesson has helped me plan for future projects.

Deciding which business entity to select for your enterprise is crucial. Will you choose an LLC, sole proprietorship, or corporation? Again, an attorney is the best person to ask to make sure you have no legal issues down the road. Once a successful search is completed, and there are no conflicts found, you should apply for your trademark and secure your brand by obtaining the website domain name and social media handles for your business. Your business name should appear the same way on all your social media pages, so you are consistent with your brand name. Keep in mind that you still will need an attorney to help you create industry-based contracts and agreements down the road once your business is fully established.

Next, you must get your tax identification number and EIN from *IRS.gov*. The process is quick, free, and accessible. You don't need to pay anyone to get your EIN. Many new business owners are taken advantage of due to a lack of knowledge. You will need your EIN to open a bank account or establish credit in your business's name. You can use this number instead of your social security number on business forms and applications. The tax identification number is a professional identifier that will help you develop and grow in the marketplace. Your EIN is used for your business, taxes, and other business transactions. You also will need to select a registered agent for your business. A registered agent is a contact person who receives official mail on behalf of your business.

Open a business bank account. Make sure to keep your incorporation forms handy because you will need them when you establish your banking relationship and other credit accounts on behalf of your business. Please make sure to keep personal transactions separate from your business transactions. This is called commingling funds. It's necessary to separate these transactions for liability and tax purposes.

You will need business tools, systems, and technology to help you maintain your enterprise. A few other vital systems include:

- *Customer relationship management system* (CRM) to organize and maintain your customers

- *Project management system* to help streamline your workflows and projects

- *Email marketing system* for communicating with your customers and clients

You may also need a platform to store your courses, coaching programs, and offers like Kajabi, Podia, or Teachable. Finally, you will need a billing system to collect funds and accounting software to keep track of all your business expenses.

Set clear goals and create a strategic plan to achieve them. Writing your goals makes them real. Mark them as completed when you have accomplished your goals. You must set weekly, monthly, quarterly, and annual goals. Just stating your goals doesn't make them materialize; you must be intentional strategically in your pursuit to accomplish your goals. Make sure to check in with your accountability partner to have a reminder in place.

Don't feel rushed during the incorporating process. The entire process may take time to get everything in order.

Always remember that you are not in this alone; you can reach out to your village for help. Organizations like the Small Business Association, National Association of Women Business Owners, and other organizations can lend a helping hand, if necessary. Organizations like the Better Business Bureau and local chambers of commerce can help establish and grow your business.

Finally, leap into entrepreneurship with a team of professionals to help you level up in business. Outside your employees, your core team should include the following business partners: an insurance agent, accountant, business coach, financial expert, intellectual property attorney, marketing & publicity expert, as well as a network of entrepreneur friends.

Build a winning team to help you conduct your endeavors. Educate your employees to lead in every area of your business. Document your corporate policies and standard operating procedures in an operation manual. Seek the advice of accountants and financial experts to assist you in setting up the appropriate investments, life insurance, and a financial plan that meets the needs of your business. Create an effective succession plan to ensure your business continues if you can no longer lead.

To become a more profitable entrepreneur, you must think of innovative ways to add more revenue to your bottom line. A fantastic way to generate more income flow into your business is to monetize your genius by creating profitable intellectual property based on your expertise. According to the Oxford English Dictionary, intellectual property is "an idea, a design, etc. that somebody has created and that the law prevents other people from copying." The best-known types are copyrights, patents, trademarks, and trade secrets." [4]Let's focus on copyrights and trademarks to add another income stream to your business. Copyrights protect your written content like books, worksheets, website content, courses, and speeches. Trademarks protect the names of your signature slogans, phrases, podcasts, courses, and coaching programs.

For instance, if you author a book based on your experience and expertise, you can provide a way to monetize your expertise and continue to build your legacy. You can reach more people and share your knowledge to educate your audience while providing more value to potential clients. Once you write a book, obtaining a copyright will provide a legal record that you are the owner of your content. So, if anyone ever infringes on your content, you can enforce your rights as the owner. You can give them notice to stop using your content without your permission by giving them a Cease and Desist notice or taking them to court to sue them for copyright infringement.

As an owner of your brand, it is essential to protect the name of your business, slogans, phrases, or program names by applying for a *trademark*. Once you obtain trademark

---

[4] See References.

ownership, you must be diligent about protecting your intellectual property. These assets can be very profitable if you strategize and create a plan to help build a legacy for your business. An intellectual property attorney can help you secure these assets for your business. Your business coach can help you monetize these assets and help you create a plan that will work for your company.

Keep learning, growing, and investing in yourself and your business. Remember to rest and reset when needed and schedule mandatory self-care throughout your journey.

CHAPTER FIVE CHECKPOINT:

1. Use your business journal that you created in chapter one to keep all the key details of your incorporation process. What kind of business do you want to have? Envision your success. Write a journal entry describing how you see your business in five years. Be descriptive.

_____

_____

_____

_____

2. Name three coaches or entrepreneurs who have your same specialty. What will make your business stand out amongst its competitors?

_____

_____

_____

_____

3. Who will be your accountability partner? How often will you meet? Will you meet in person or virtually?

_____

_____

_____

_____

Chapter Six

Launch Your Dream & Start Planning Your Exit!

"Fly Fearlessly Into Your God-given Purpose!"

Everyone's entrepreneurial journey looks different. One person may be happy with having a part-time enterprise; meanwhile, another person may want to be a full-time entrepreneur. The timeframe to transition from employee to full-time entrepreneur will vary based on each person. It comes down to being mentally prepared for the entrepreneurship difficulties that lie ahead. Let's face it. One of the most significant challenges when transitioning from employee to entrepreneur is having enough money to sustain and live within your current lifestyle.

In the beginning stages, the business may be slow. Don't be so quick to leave your 9 to 5 if your business is not making two to three times your current salary. If you have not prepared a way to attract qualified leads, and you don't have a continuous flow of convertible leads, how will you get clients for your business? You must have a way to bring clients into your business, so you are able to provide your services and make money in your business.

Remember that you want to keep your same standard of living or better than when you were working your 9 to 5. If you're the primary breadwinner for your family, you want to make sure you can pay all your bills and have extra funds set aside in case emergencies occur. If possible, you want to save at least a couple of years salary or more just in case unforeseen events happen.

A significant thing to remember is when you're transitioning from employee to entrepreneur, pace yourself. This process is a marathon, not a sprint. Don't compare your entrepreneurial journey to someone else's entrepreneurial journey. Depending on your responsibilities, it may take years to transition from an employee to a full-time entrepreneur. You still could work your 9 to 5 and be a part-time entrepreneur. You need to be okay with this fact. Don't feel pressured to transition to a full-time entrepreneurship too early if your finances don't allow you to do that.

It's so vital that you do not compare your journey to someone else's journey.

Try not to fall into the comparison trap, especially by just viewing someone's social media pages. A lot of people are on social media promoting their highlight reels, but they are not showing their challenges and struggles. Just know that you are right where you are supposed to be. With hard work, consistency, dedication, and the help you need, you will be where you need to be to pull this entrepreneurship journey together! Tap into your network of new and seasoned business owners to have a tribe of professionals cheering you on as you grow into the female boss you are meant to be!

Let your 9 to 5 finance your entrepreneurial goals and dreams. Remember, you don't have to do everything all at once. You can do things little by little. Just put a plan of action in place. Think about the things you need for your business: computer equipment, legal fees, business coaching fees, supplies, business and health insurance, payroll and taxes. You will need to create a budget to plan out all the things that you need for full-time entrepreneurship.

Plans are great, but you must put the ideas into action. *Align your goals with action.* You will have a business and a marketing plan, but before leaping into full-time entrepreneurship, create a checklist of things you want to accomplish. Once the checklist has been completed, you will be ready to retire from corporate America and pursue entrepreneurship fully. If your goals are being met, give yourself a retirement date and start marking the days on the calendar to signify that you are approaching it.

For instance, if you have any major purchases lined up like a home, you may want to make that purchase before you leave corporate America. The first few years may be challenging, which may result in the delay of significant purchases like a home because you will have to show at least two years of stable earnings. Also, remember that most businesses show a loss for the first few years. If you are showing losses, then it may be hard to substantiate your income.

I want to reiterate the importance of maintaining your champion mindset. You must be able to manage the rejection you may face as a new business owner. There may be tough obstacles that will show up randomly. These situations may shift your mindset into thinking that you have made a mistake by leaving a stable, promising, and paying career. If you have unresolved issues, they will rear their ugly head in your business. In the initial stages of your business, you may become frustrated if things are not panning out as you imagined. These experiences make it easy for you to give up. Many times, it's just growing pains. You must remain levelheaded and stick in there.

Finally, you must empower yourself to win! You must believe without any doubt that you can make your entrepreneurial dreams a reality. If you can visualize your success, it can happen. It would be best if you had a proven strategy that yields success. Have a solid business process and work with a business coach to solidify your success strategy.

Optimize your power plan, consistently evaluate the market, and ensure that you meet your ideal client's needs. You can gain a loyal base of happy clients when you meet your clients' needs. Delighted customers usually refer more people to your business because you operate in excellence. People are happy to spread the word about your services when you are doing an excellent job and solving a significant pain point for them.

If you have a high-quality product or service, and your ideal client's needs are being met, you will be successful. If you are visible in the community and have a winning mindset, you will be successful. You have to remember to never give up and accomplish the goals that you set for your business. If, for any reason, you are not successful, never be ashamed to go back to your 9 to 5 until you are ready to leap back into entrepreneurship. Don't feel like you have failed because you've put 100% into your dream of being your boss.

Sometimes, you may need to tweak a few things and seek the experience of a successful mentor or coach. Once you have established your business, set clear attainable goals, accomplished them, and created a signature business blueprint for success, you'll be unstoppable!

Preparing to exit corporate America takes strategic planning. First, you want to select your retirement date. Be sure to give yourself enough time to save money for living expenses and insurance, apply for grants, and make other important business decisions. Don't be too anxious to leave corporate America until you have done the following five things:

1. Seek the advice of a financial advisor to help you maintain your current lifestyle, secure life insurance, and secure supplemental plans as well as your 401k investment account. When you leave corporate America, you lose the matching contributions from your previous employer. You must be able to continue saving for your retirement. It would help if you also created a way to keep contributing to your funds to remain on track with your retirement savings. It's essential to select a knowledgeable financial expert who can help you avoid penalties or taxes for early withdrawals from your retirement account.

2. As a licensed insurance agent with over two decades' worth of experience, I know the importance of doing your due diligence and researching your options to secure the best health insurance plan for your family. Many people put their retirement or entrepreneurship on hold until they

better grasp their future health insurance costs. Multiple options are available including the Consolidated Omnibus Budget Reconciliation Act (COBRA), which is a continuation of your current health plan for up to 18 months.

Check with local independent insurance brokers who can shop rates and find the best plan for you. As another option, you can contact local health insurance carriers directly and ask for a quote to see if you can find a plan to meet your health insurance needs. Make sure you can keep your same doctors and hospitals. Remember that once you leave your employer, you'll have a sixty-day special enrollment period to obtain health insurance. After that time period, you may have to wait until the annual open enrollment period, typically from November 1st to December 15th for individuals under age of 65. For Medicare-eligible individuals, your annual election period is from October 15-December 7th annually. Outside that timeframe, you will have to wait until open enrollment for the following year unless you have experienced a recent qualifying life event within the past sixty days like marriage, the birth of a child, or a permanent move. Since you will be self-employed, you want to re-evaluate your situation and see if you qualify for subsidies within the health insurance marketplace. Visit healthcare.gov for more information.

3. Don't be afraid to get outside your comfort zone and take risks. There will be many risky situations during your

entrepreneurship journey. Sometimes, you will be confronted with making some critical decisions that may determine if you will or will not make it in business. Therefore, you must pack your patience, pray, and lean into everything you know and love to make the best decisions for the betterment of your business.

4. Keep reading relevant books, learning, and growing by investing in yourself and your business. Attend workshops and conferences to continually hone your niche and immediately incorporate any new things you've learned. Personal development will be a critical factor in your growth and champion mindset.

5. Remember to rest and reset when needed. Schedule mandatory self-care breaks when necessary. Set boundaries, guard your time, and never be afraid to say "no" when others ask for you to overextend yourself when you are fully booked. Ask for help when needed.

CHAPTER SIX CHECKPOINT

1. How long will it take to transition to entrepreneurship? Consider your current obligations and lifestyle. What will you do to ensure that you can maintain your current responsibilities?

_____

_____

_____

_____

2. How will you manage obstacles during the initial stages of your business? Do you plan to visit a mental health professional to help you deal with the difficulties of entrepreneurship, or will you have an accountability partner who understands what you are going through as a new business owner?

_____

_____

_____

_____

3. How do you plan to let people know about your business? How does your marketing plan look? How will you ensure that you can convert leads to your business?

_____

_____

_____

_____

Chapter Seven

Activate, Maintain & Sustain!

"You are a major influencer dominating your niche!"

N ow that you have done the necessary personal, professional, and mindset work, it's time to level up again, pull all your resources together, and create a plan to activate your purpose in business. It's time to build, maintain, and carry your brilliance into the next generation. You must create a plan that will continue to sustain and build generational wealth.

Creating a recession-proof business will enable you to make a profit in your enterprise regardless of the economy's decline. Your business idea must make you stand out from your competitors. Consistently communicating with your clients will help you to stay top of mind; this way, you will always know what they need from you as a business. Use this insight to your advantage, provide the service and serve it up to them on a platter. Keep tweaking your process until you get it right.

Investing in coaching has allowed me to grow personally as an author, speaker, and coach. I value the importance of investing in my growth as a business professional. Since the beginning stages of my business, I always have sought the experience of experts to help me get to the next level. Collaborating with experienced coaches has allowed me to glean from their previous experience and avoid novice mistakes.

Build a solid foundation for your company by creating a company mission, vision, and values. Create your business code of conduct that will guide all business activities within your organization. Start mentoring your children and trusted family members, so they can take over the company when you are ready for retirement. Incorporating family early on is an essential part of the wealth-building plan.

Document these company standards in a business manual. Write out business wants and needs. Create your customers' journey by mapping out their entire experience from the beginning to the end. This pathway shows the customers' first interaction and each touchpoint they experienced that allowed them to become loyal clients.

Document everything that you integrate into your business. Be very consistent with how you oversee everything in your business. When you create something new for your business, test everything out. Get feedback from your target audience. Always ask your customers what they want and serve it on a silver platter. Tweak it and take it to market. Build it. Sustain it. Scale it. Continue to build your business brand. Utilize your past experiences to create a stellar experience for your customers that will make them become loyal clients. Identify areas where you need to develop and grow.

I SURVEYED SEVERAL BUSINESSWOMEN ON FACEBOOK ABOUT HOW THEY MAINTAIN SUCCESS IN THEIR BUSINESSES. HERE'S WHAT THEY SAID:

1. Kimberly Richardson said she maintains success in her business by "Walking in my calling."

2. Precious "Killerpitchmaster" Williams said she maintains success "With God, prayer, a support network of those who keep me accountable, having solid goals and a team that does not quit!"

3. Sylvia Hubbard-Hutula stated that "Consistency" will help you sustain your success.

4. Sonya Davis stated that she "maintains by having my mentors in place as well as consistently improving my mindset."

5. Tinisha Poitier said, "It is vital to be a quick action taker. Follow expert advice, meditate, implementation, implementation, implementation!"

6. Brandy Jackson stated, "I utilize my calendar HEAVY. I plan out my week and dig down deeper into each day by placing a time with the tasks. I teach my mentees these tips as well."

Stay relevant in your niche by doing these four things.

1. Author a book highlighting your expertise. Use the content from your book to create a coaching program, courses, or consulting business to teach others about your subject matter.

2. Read current research journals in your field and stay on top of contemporary trends in your field of study.

3. Become a thought leader in your expertise. Host events, speak at conferences, author articles, be a guest on podcasts or the media, and share your industry knowledge.

4. Create industry-related content and post it on social media. Engage with your target audience and provide specialized tools, tips, and resources that are important in your industry.

Leveraging your relationships within your networks will help spread the word about your business and help you sustain success. Dominate your expertise. Become the brand your client needs. Then, decide what's next. Remember to celebrate every victory. Keep growing, keep building, and *skyrocket your success*!

CHAPTER SEVEN CHECKPOINT

1. How will you build a recession-proof business that will extend beyond this generation?

_____

_____

_____

_____

2. How will you maintain and sustain your business success?

_____

_____

_____

_____

3. How will you branch out and become a thought leader in your niche?

_____

_____

_____

_____

Notes

Epilogue

Congratulations! You are an entrepreneurial woman operating in your purpose! You have completed this road map, so you can transition into entrepreneurship successfully. Reading this book has provided several strategies to elevate your mindset, boost your confidence, own your genius, and thrive in a female-led enterprise! I'm so proud of you! Anything you want is within your reach; all you have to do is *visualize it, write your plan, and activate your mission*.

When you take action, a whole new world will open up limitless possibilities and opportunities that will catapult you to the higher level of success you have been dreaming about. You will gain more freedom in your thinking and your lifestyle.

Let's recap what you've learned by reading *Skyrocket Your Success 2.0: The Corporate Women's Road Map to Navigate from Employee to Entrepreneur*. The following is a summary of what was taught in this book.

Chapter 1. This chapter helps you to recognize and acknowledge that you are not where you want to be in life. It helps you to recognize that there is a life of career fulfillment

SKYROCKET YOUR SUCCESS 2.0!

waiting for you. You don't have to be complacent in corporate America when you are called to be an entrepreneur. Assess your current situation and discover that there are new business opportunities in which you can monetize your skills and continue to build your legacy!

Chapter 2. Assess your skill set, identify where you shine, know your value, and tap into your zone of genius. Create a plan to monetize your expertise in the marketplace.

Chapter 3. Elevating your mindset helps you to diffuse all the self-doubt and the imposter syndrome you may be feeling as you boost your confidence by affirming the value of your skills, experience, and abilities.

Chapter 4. Redefine your success journey. You don't have to be stuck in an unfulfilled routine job when you can take what you know and thrive. Envision a new life on your terms as you create a new definition of success.

Chapter 5. Incorporate and build your winning team. Make your business official and assemble an enterprising team to help you accomplish your business goals.

Chapter 6. Navigate from corporate America into entrepreneurship with grace. It's not a race and transition into full-time entrepreneurship when you are ready. Successfully segue into entrepreneurship by creating a plan that will allow you to transition smoothly and confidently.

Chapter 7. Activate, sustain, and maintain your business by setting reasonable goals. Scale and grow your business with the help of proven successful business coaches to help you soar. Build your legacy and a succession plan to sustain your business for your future generations.

You have all the keys to succeed. You have the knowledge, ability, confidence, and grace to make it happen! Your tribe is waiting for you. Pursue your greatness and *Skyrocket Your Success!*

References

- Chapter 2, Ecclesiastes 3:1: Scripture quotations marked "NLT" New Living Translation Holy Bible, New Living Translation, copyright © 1996, 2004, 2015 by Tyndale House Foundation. Used by permission of Tyndale House Publishers, Inc., Carol Stream, Illinois 60188. All rights reserved.

- Chapter 3, "Emotional Intelligence" Oxford English Dictionary 2023. Oxford University Press. https://www.oxfordlearnersdictionaries.com/us/definition/american english/emotional-intelligence?q=emotional+intelligence (10 January 2023.)

- Chapter 4, "The Success Factor Survey", SKYROCKET YOUR SUCCESS! 10 Keys to Refocus, Reposition, & Reclaim Your Purpose! Copyright 2019 © by Queashar L. Halliburton used by permission of QUEASHAR DETROIT PUBLISHING, LLC, Ferndale, MI 48220. All Rights Reserved.

- Chapter 5, "Intellectual Property" Oxford English Dictionary 2023. Oxford University Press. https://www.oxfordlearnersdictionaries.com/us/definition/english/int ellectual-property?q=intellectual+property (10 January 2023.)

I hope this book has motivated, inspired, and empowered you to move forward and continue to pursue your entrepreneurial goals. If you enjoyed *Skyrocket Your Success 2.0*, please feel free to leave a 5-star review on Amazon.

If you would like the companion workbook for Skyrocket Your Success 2.0, or if you want more information regarding speaking and coaching opportunities, please contact Queashar Halliburton at hello@sharhalliburton.com.

Stay connected with Queashar on the following social media platforms:

Facebook: www.facebook.com/qdpublishing
LinkedIn: www.linkedin.com/in/queasharhalliburton
Twitter: www.twitter.com/qdpublishing
Instagram: www.instagram.com/qdpublishing
Amazon Author Central:
https://www.amazon.com/author/queasharhalliburton

About The Author

Although many abandon their goals and dreams due to fear, uncertainty, procrastination, and insufficient resources, she turns each of those things into stepping stones to her success.

For Queashar L. Halliburton, CEO and founder of *QUEASHAR DETROIT PUBLISHING* ®, her most significant success to date resulted from living outside the box and operating in her God-given gifts and purpose. While producing her fair share of best-selling literary works, Queashar diligently positions new authors nationwide to tell their stories with clarity, character, and distinction.

Queashar has been featured in *Speakers* Magazine, *Courageous Woman* Magazine, *Glambitious* Magazine, and *Voyage* Michigan. In addition to serving as a member of the Black Speakers Network and the Nonfiction Authors Association, Queashar is a contributing writer for *Advance* Magazine and *Publish* Magazine.

Book Queashar as a speaker for your next women's conference at https://sharhalliburton.com.

www.ingramcontent.com/pod-product-compliance
Lightning Source LLC
Chambersburg PA
CBHW020326130626
46549CB00003B/1036